LIFE LESSONS
I LEARNED

FROM MY CAT

Illustrated by Jamie Shelman

First published in Great Britain in 2018 by LOM ART, and imprint of
Michael O'Mara Books Limited
9 Lion Yard
Tremadoc Road
London SW4 7NQ

Illustration copyright © Jamie Shelman
Text copyright © Michael O'Mara Books Ltd

A CIP catalogue record for this book is available
from the British Library.

Papers used by Michael O'Mara Books Limited are natural,
recyclable products made from wood grown in sustainable
forests. The manufacturing processes conform to the
environmental regulations of the country of origin.

ISBN: 978-1-910552-91-9 in hardback print format
ISBN: 978-1-910552-97-1 in ebook format

3 5 7 9 10 8 6 4

Designed and typeset by Claire Cater

Printed and bound in China

Follow us on Twitter @OMaraBooks

www.mombooks.com

DEDICATED TO MY NEIGHBOUR'S CAT,
BROOKSY, WHO WAITS FOR US EVERY
MORNING AT OUR WINDOW

I have loved and lived with many cats throughout my life and know there are many life lessons to be learned from watching our feline friends. From how to live, love and get what you want, to being at peace with oneself and knowing what matters most in life ... food, sleep and a little companionship!

In this fast-paced, distracted world, I find myself now more than ever turning to cats (mostly my neighbour's, Brooksy) for comfort, quietude, joy and even a little guidance. Cats are wise and silly, needy and aloof, simple and unique – and oh-so-brilliant at being content doing nothing. I hope that in this book you can recognize some of the lessons learned from your own cat and that one day we can all learn to sit perfectly still, eyes squinted with pleasure, content until the next meal!

Jamie

STRETCH REGULARLY

GET PLENTY OF REST

... BECAUSE NAPS ARE
NEVER TO BE ASHAMED OF

STAY WARM

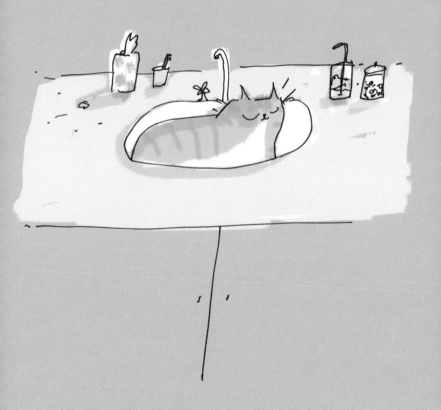

ENJOY YOUR QUIET TIME

MAINTAIN A WELL-
GROOMED APPEARANCE

EAT MORE FISH

SOAK UP
THE SUN

ONLY EAT WHAT YOU WANT

WASH WHEN YOU CAN

A BEAUTIFUL MANE
TAKES SERIOUS WORK

... AND SO DOES THE
PERFECT SET OF NAILS

BE AN EARLY RISER

... BUT IT'S OKAY TO STAY
IN BED A LITTLE BIT LONGER

DAYDREAM

SPEAK UP AND USE YOUR VOICE

CONSERVE YOUR ENERGY

THINK

OUTSIDE

THE BOX

BE PATIENT ...

... AND KEEP YOUR EYE ON THE PRIZE

LEARN THE ART OF NEGOTIATION

BE DIRECT

GIVE POSITIVE FEEDBACK

MAKE EYE CONTACT

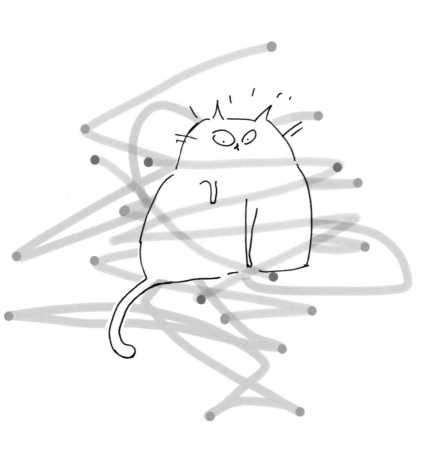

DON'T BE DISCOURAGED

DON'T
WORK TOO
HARD

BE ESPECIALLY ATTENTIVE
TO THE ONE PERSON IN THE
ROOM WHO DOESN'T LIKE YOU

BE PLEASED WITH YOUR
ACHIEVEMENTS, HOWEVER SMALL

PURRFECT YOUR DEATH STARE

PURRFECT YOUR POKER FACE

MAKE

YOUR

MARK

WALK WITH (C)ATTITUDE

... AND KEEP THE CLAWS SHARP

STAY FOCUSED

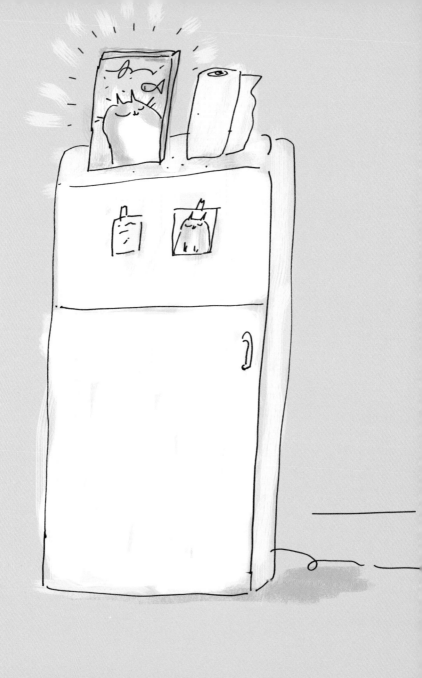

ONCE YOU'VE MADE UP YOUR MIND,
DON'T CHANGE IT

AIM HIGH

THE BEST SOLUTION TO A
PROBLEM IS A NAP

ANXIETY IS NOTHING TO BE ASHAMED OF

LIVE IN THE MOMENT

BE RESILIENT

DON'T SWEAT THE SMALL STUFF

BEING ANTI-SOCIAL IS OKAY

TAKE TIME TO REFLECT

CONFRONT YOUR FEARS

SLOW DOWN

EXERCISE ONLY WHEN YOU FEEL LIKE IT

LIVE OUTSIDE OF YOUR COMFORT ZONE

NOTHING IS PERSONAL

IRRATIONAL FEARS ARE NORMAL

MAKE THE MOST OF
WHAT YOU'VE GOT

DRINKING WATER IS GOOD FOR THE SOUL

LOOK AFTER YOURSELF FIRST

DON'T BE AFRAID TO LET
SOMEONE KNOW YOU LIKE THEM

ALWAYS LOOK PLEASED WHEN
THEY COME THROUGH THE DOOR

BE WHO YOU ARE
AND THE RIGHT
PERSON WILL
LOVE YOU FOR IT

BE GOOD AT RECEIVING AFFECTION

BUT DON'T BE NEEDY

STAY AT LEAST TEN FEET AWAY FROM
YOUR LOVED ONE AT ALL TIMES

WOMEN AND CATS WILL DO AS THEY PLEASE

... AND MEN AND DOGS SHOULD RELAX
AND GET USED TO IT

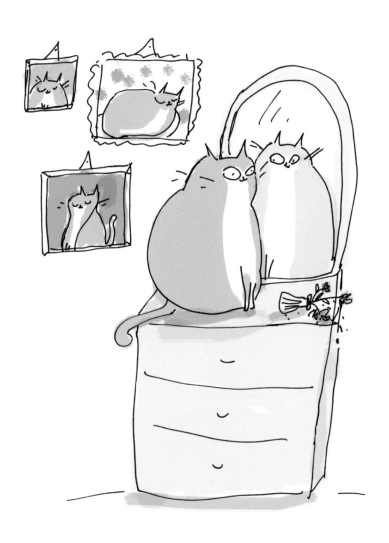

LOVE YOURSELF FIRST

ACCEPT LOVE ON YOUR OWN TERMS

IGNORE ANYONE WHO DOESN'T WORSHIP YOU

LOOK BEFORE YOU LEAP

NEVER TRUST A MAN WHO DOESN'T LIKE CATS

TRUST YOUR INTUITION

BE CURIOUS

BE YOURSELF

BE INDEPENDENT

BE ELUSIVE

SOMETIMES YOU WILL
LEAP AND FALL ...

... BUT YOU CAN LAND
ON YOUR FEET

TEST THE

BOUNDARIES

PRESERVE YOUR DIGNITY AT ALL TIMES

BE A GOOD LISTENER

MAKE THE MOST OF YOUR NINE LIVES

EXPLORE THE WORLD

NAP ANYWHERE

LOOK AT THINGS FROM A
DIFFERENT PERSPECTIVE

DON'T WORRY WHAT
OTHERS THINK OF YOU

A HISS IS WORTH A
THOUSAND WORDS

BE EASILY ENTERTAINED

GET AWAY
WITH MURDER
BY LOOKING
CUTE

BE THE CENTRE OF ATTENTION
AT WHATEVER COST

THERE'S NOTHING BETTER
THAN A GOOD BOOK

LEARN TO MAKE YOURSELF COMFORTABLE WHEREVER YOU ARE

NEVER LOSE YOUR PLAYFULNESS

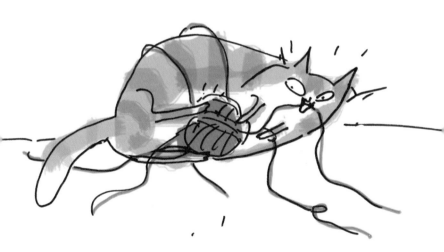

STAND YOUR GROUND

BE TAKEN
ON YOUR
OWN TERMS

ALWAYS GIVE GENEROUSLY

CHOOSE YOUR FRIENDS WISELY

BE SILLY ... AND OFTEN

KEEP YOUR ENEMIES CLOSE

EMBRACE

YOUR

WEIRD

BE TOLERANT OF CHILDREN

CELEBRATE FAMILY MEALTIMES

IF YOU WANT SOMEONE'S ATTENTION,

SIT IN FRONT OF THE TV

ALWAYS DEFEND YOUR HOME

A CHAOTIC HOME IS A HAPPY HOME

DON'T BE AFRAID OF MICE

NEVER LET

ANYONE

DRESS YOU

THE BEST SEAT IN THE
HOUSE IS THE ONE SOMEONE
IS ALREADY SITTING ON